IMAGES OF WALES

AROUND
GILWERN

IMAGES OF WALES

AROUND GILWERN

DAVID EDGE

TEMPUS

This book is dedicated to the memory of Robert William Edge (1934-1991), who loved the county of Breconshire.

Frontispiece: On Easter Monday 1986 a football match was played between High Trees Road, Gilwern and Orchard Close, Gilwern. The High Trees Road team pose for the camera before kick-off. From left to right, back row: Jonathan Hardwick, Greg Powell, Julian Hardwick, Ashley Cooper, Geoff Williams, David Miles. Front row: Andrew Packer, David Edge, John Phillips, Stephen Waller.

First published 2004, reprinted 2005

Tempus Publishing Limited
The Mill, Brimscombe Port,
Stroud, Gloucestershire, GL5 2QG
www.tempus-publishing.com

© David Edge, 2004

The right of David Edge to be identified as the Author
of this work has been asserted in accordance with the
Copyrights, Designs and Patents Act 1988.

British Library Cataloguing in Publication Data.
A catalogue record for this book is available from the British Library.

ISBN 0 7524 3285 0

Typesetting and origination by Tempus Publishing Limited.
Printed in Great Britain.

Contents

Acknowledgements   6

Introduction   7

one   The Canal   9

two   Gilwern   23

three   The Congregational Chapel, Gilwern   43

four   Clydach   55

five   The Railway   79

six   Brynmawr Comprehensive School   95

seven   Gilwern Cubs   117

Acknowledgements

I would like to thank everyone who has helped in compiling this book, by lending photographs, giving advice and proof reading. I would also like to thank my wife Janette for her endless patience as the book came together, along with Clive Boulter, Richard M. Casserley, Anne Eynon, Jack Evans, Lesley Flynn, M. Hale, Carol Hopkins, Les Knight, Mary James (*née* Moss), Myddyn and Ellien Jones, Sandra Jones (*née* Evans), Nigel Lewis, Larry and Betty Thomas, Howard Williams, Mike Miles, Mr and Mrs Dennis Moss, Gladys Turley, Kathleen and Jim Parker. I would also like to record a special thanks to my life-long friends Sue and Nigel Arnold and Nicholas Seabourne, without whose help this book would not have been possible. The omission of any names or any infringement of copyright are entirely unintentional.

Introduction

I have always had an interest in history, possibly because my father was a history teacher and local history has always fascinated me. The villages of Gilwern and Clydach are steeped in local history, legend and myth. Stories from many years ago have sometimes been embellished to expand the facts. Nevertheless, the truth is that to many people the village, town or city in which they grew up will always have a special place in their heart. This is particularly true in my case.

I came to live in the village of Gilwern in October 1961 with my parents and younger sister Sian. We moved into a three-bedroom house, which was then newly built in the main street. Mr and Mrs Bill Turner and their children Elizabeth and David were our first acquaintances. Later Mr and Mrs Myddyn Jones moved next door with their children Michael and Anthony. At that time Gilwern was a small village which was growing slowly. The building of the Heads of the Valleys Road was in progress but at the time the traffic came through the village. I was undoubtedly inquisitive as a child and as I grew I began to explore the village and outlying areas.

In September 1962 an event occurred which was truly unforgettable to all concerned. This was my first day at school. I should have guessed something was up when I was smartly dressed by my mother, given one of my favourite toys and together with my best friend Anthony, taken for a short walk. On arriving at a strange building I joined a number of children, both boys and girls, in a largish room: my new school and my new classmates. After being introduced to the teacher (Miss Walters, a typical schoolmistress of the old guard – formidable, fearsome and competent) we were left in her care.

Miss Walters had many years' experience in teaching and was well used to dealing with a new intake of children. However, she was not prepared for the events that followed. Within seconds of all the parents leaving many of the children, myself included, began to cry and soon there was a crescendo of noise. Some children began to dash towards the door, in a desperate bid for freedom and home. Miss Walters was bravely trying to stop these escapes and seemed to have eight arms as she bravely repelled all attempts. Years of experience had taught her that after ten or fifteen minutes things would settle down. However, on this day she got it wrong as escape attempts were still being made over an hour later. By now Miss Walters was beginning to tire and in a valiant effort to subdue the wailing children she was forced to lock the door. I must confess to being as bad as the rest and like all the others my escape attempts failed. This tragic day ended at 3.15 p.m., the torment for teacher, parents and children finally ending.

My grandfather recorded the end of this day on cine film, which sadly has not been seen for over thirty years. The first year in Gilwern Primary School was not my best and I often got into trouble with Miss Walters. However, as at my next school, once the first year was over things improved. By the time I came to my last year at Gilwern when I was a pupil in standard four, under the control of Mr Lance Jones, I was quite enjoying myself. The headmaster during my time at Gilwern School was Mr Hopkins, a strict but fair man, who had the ability to terrify you with a mesmerising, and sometimes frightening, stare. Sadly it has not been possible to incorporate pictures of the school in this volume. During my time at Gilwern School I made many friends and it is not possible to mention them all; however I should mention Simon Ambler, Robert McKelvie, Nigel Hanney and Christopher Fox with whom I spent many years playing in and around the village.

Between 1969 and 1974 I attended Brynmawr Comprehensive School where I made other friends. As we became teenagers the playing changed to the interests of all teenagers which included football, rugby and, of course, girls. Again it is not possible to mention everyone but I should include Christopher and Wayne Owens, Stephen Harris, Gillian Hardwick, Carol Joynson, Carol Morris and Sally Anne Watkins. My family moved to Clydach in 1973 where I remained until I moved away in 1982. I have very fond memories of growing up in Gilwern and Clydach and since those early days I have seen many changes to both villages and the surrounding area.

During the time I lived in Gilwern and Clydach, a period of around twenty years, memorable events included the Queen's visit to Gilwern in 1963; the time when a caravan became detached from its car, crashing into the Congregational Chapel in Gilwern's main street; and the day the Milk Race came through. Today both Gilwern and Clydach are dormitory towns where people live but more often than not commute to places such as Newport, Cardiff or Bristol.

I hope that this book will revive happy memories and although I have covered subjects which are of particular interest to me, I realize that there are areas that have not been mentioned perhaps a second book will follow. Every chapter illustrates the changes which have taken place, but these have all been in the name of progress. I have many fond memories of the area in which I grew up and I trust the reader will enjoy this book.

David Edge

one

The Canal

Gilwern village, before 1974 in the county of Breconshire and since 2003 in the county of Monmouthshire, has always been a favourite summer spot visited by pleasure parties and tourists. The village enjoys a splendid situation and picturesque surroundings. It stands on the slopes of the hill, along which, until its closure in 1958, ran the former London & North Western Railway, which operated between Abergavenny and Merthyr Tydfil. Until the opening of the Heads of the Valleys Road in the early 1960s, the main road from Brynmawr passed along the main street of the village to Abergavenny.

The Brecknock and Abergavenny canal crossed the valley through the village, and adds much interest and pleasure for visitors and local inhabitants alike. As early as 1905 a trip on a pleasure boat to Llangattock, four miles away, was delightful. The thick foliage along the banks, broken occasionally by the opening glades along the way, combined with the birds and flowers, surely presented a wonderful scene to the people of that time. This photograph provides an overview of Gilwern village, taken possibly around 1930 from Gilwern Mountain. At that time the housing estates of Bryn Glas and Orchard Close had in all probability not even been considered; Bryn Glas was built in the early 1950s and Orchard Close around 1960.

Above and below: Two photographs of the picturesque canal in the village of Gilwern. A large part of the canal's route lies within the Brecon Beacons National Park. As the canal approaches Gilwern from the village of Govilon it meanders across the valley, giving an air of peace and tranquillity. The walk along the canal towards Church Road was once along a stony footpath, and the canal curved around Gilwern village passing the old house at Clydach Wharf (also known locally as Gilwern basin), which was later demolished. This is the view of the boating shed in the village circa 1920. The shed was still in use in the 1960s under the control of Mr Price from the Roadhouse Café. Mr Price operated a number of rowing boats for hire. Many a young lad assisted Mr Price in operating the boats and often fell into the canal. Before Mr Price, Mr Gooding had owned and operated the boats. Gilwern School can be seen in the distance of the lower picture. A date of 1912 could be found on one of the buildings indicating when the school was built. To reach the school a walk from the main road along School Lane was required.

We should not forget that in the eighteenth century canals were a modern and a very effective means of transport and the purpose of the Brecknock and Abergavenny Canal was to carry local goods and products to places such as Newport. The canal was proposed in 1792, which the history books record as the canal mania era. Major canal building would appear to have been between 1759 and 1845, which is when both the agricultural and industrial revolutions were taking place. To complete this remarkable feat of engineering (towards the final destination of Newport), a total distance of 42 miles, 116 bridges were built. Also required were six locks and a number of aqueducts. Here we see a number of people enjoying a day's boating on the canal in around 1920.

This interesting photograph of the frozen canal in 1917 shows tree trunks ready for transportation. As the First World War was at its height they may have been destined for the war effort in France.

The Rectory, on the left-hand side of the photograph, was the home of the Rector of the parish church of Llanelly. This fine church stands on the breast of the hill approximately one mile away from Gilwern village, facing the Usk Valley and commands a fine view of arguably the most beautiful countryside in Wales.

The parish church of Llanelly had been known at one time as St Elli and was originally built in the twelfth century.

Rectory and Canal, Gilwern. (Winter.)

Temple's Series

Above: This picture shows the tunnel of the Clydach Railroad, which ran under the canal through the Gilwern embankment. Built in 1794 by John Dadford, the railroad predated the canal and ran from Gelli Felen to Glangrwyney.

Opposite above: The canal basin at Gilwern around 1920, showing a winter scene which people from older generations will remember as commonplace prior to the onset of global warming. To the left of the picture is Clydach wharf, which at one time was the hub of activity for the loading of cargo onto the barges. From around 1800 until the railway came to the village during the 1860s, lime, iron and coal were transported from this location. The destinations were in Herefordshire, Radnorshire and the port of Newport.

Opposite below: Sunday School outings on the canal from the local churches and chapels were popular, as can be seen from this photograph.

This photograph shows what was once known as Dadford's great embankment, and we see the River Clydach which runs under the canal. This is where the canal construction began in 1797. John Dadford had surveyed the route of the canal and in 1798 he became the full-time engineer on the project.

A summer view of the canal on top of the embankment, a short distance away from Gilwern's main street, around 1974.

CANAL GILWERN. BREC.

The canal near to Gilwern basin, around 1960, by now only used for pleasure boats. The house seen on the right was demolished around 1964. By this time the canal had been around for over 150 years, and the fact that it had been built with only picks, shovels and wheelbarrows may have been forgotten by many of the visitors to the area at that time.

This picture, taken in 1982, shows a housing estate known as Malford Grove on the left as well as evidence of considerable work carried out on the canal path. The trees on the right of the picture have grown considerably since the early 1960s and are beginning to hide Auckland House (a fine building with enchanting gardens which slope towards the canal) and the disused lime kilns. The rebuilt bridge can be seen in the background. Numbered 104 it is also known in some circles as Auckland Bridge and was rebuilt in 1973 from the old standard stone humpback style to the more modern style. Church Road is now considerably wider than in 1960 and carries much more traffic. A walk of no more than 400 yards would bring visitors to the Corn Exchange public house at the bottom of the hill.

Opposite below: Here we see bridge 106 as the Brecknock and Abergavenny canal continues on its journey towards Brecon. The overhanging trees add to the aura of peace and tranquillity, reminding us of a bygone age when life was less hectic. In 1880 the control of both canals was taken over by the Great Western Railway.

Right: Views of the canal as it meanders its way towards Brecon, leaving the village of Gilwern about a mile behind. In order to transport goods between Brecon and Newport by canal, the working boats would need to travel along two canals. The termination of the Brecknock and Abergavenny canal was at Pontymoile, 33 miles from Brecon. From Pontymoile to Newport the barges travelled on the Monmouthshire canal, the distance being 9 miles. The Act of Parliament authorizing the construction of the Monmouthshire canal was passed in 1792.

Canal & Woods Gilwern

The Drawbridge, Govilon, Nr Abergavenny. 522.

We should not forget the fact that in the eighteenth century canals were the equivalent of today's motorways and a very effective means of transporting goods and produce. The canal was built between 1797 and 1800. *Above:* The Drawbridge at Govilon is approximately a mile and a half away from Gilwern. *Below:* the Clydach basin and the old wharf to the right, as the canal meanders left towards Gilwern village.

The Canal & Gilwern Hill, Gilwern.

Above: This house, known as The Cwm and still standing today, is close to the Clydach Railroad which is on the right of the photograph, and behind the canal at Clydach Wharf. Machine House on the Maesygwartha Road, built in around 1810, can be seen at the top in the centre of the photograph. Sadly, the date is not known.

Below: This fine postcard dated around 1910 gives five excellent views of Gilwern. The canal features in three of the five pictures and the long leisurely walks and boating trips no doubt gave as much pleasure as taking a trip to Disneyworld today.

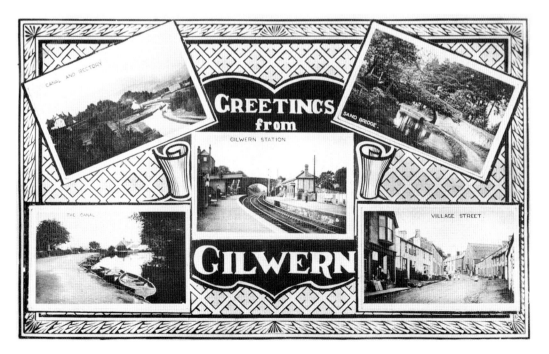

A fine view of Powells boathouse at Llangattock should remind us that it was the passing of an Act of Parliament in 1793 that allowed work on the Brecknock and Abergavenny canal to begin. As with many canals throughout Great Britain, the decline of commercial traffic meant that the canal could not remain profitable and this resulted in the British Transport Commission taking control of canals in 1947 under the Transport Act of that year. In 1963 the control of canals was passed to the British Waterways Board (a new name for the British Transport Commission). Five years later in 1968 an agreement was reached between Monmouthshire and Breconshire County Council, in conjunction with the British Waterways Board, for future restoration of the canal. Each County Council agreed to bear half the cost of the work.

The canal has come a long way in two hundred years and remains as popular as ever. This British Waterways advertisement is from 1973.

two

Gilwern

Above: Sir Henry Edward Bartle Frere was born in 1815, some records indicating at Ty Mawr House, Gilwern. His life included some notable achievements. His father Edward Frere was born at Clydach House. After attending King Edward Grammar School in Bath he progressed to Haileybury College to complete his studies. He entered the Bombay Civil Service in 1834 and later achieved the position of Secretary to the Governor of Bombay. He learnt to speak a number of languages, including Hindi, Marathi and Gujarati. In 1850 he became Governor of Scinde and in 1859 received the Companionship of the Bath together with the thanks of both Houses of Parliament. Sir Henry became the Governor of Bombay in 1862. Returning to Britain in 1867 he became a member of Her Majesty's Privy Council in 1873 and was the Grand Commander of the Bath and a baronet by 1876. He was acclaimed as a man of exceptional ability, and after his death on 29 May 1884 he was laid to rest in St Paul's Cathedral. In Kenya, the town of Frere is named after him and on the Thames Embankment stands a memorial to him. Two of the eminent positions Sir Henry held during his lifetime were President of the Royal Geographical Society and Vice President of the Society for Spreading the Gospel in Foreign Parts. Both Oxford and Cambridge honoured him with the title of Doctor of Law. Sadly, he is also remembered for helping to start the Zulu war.

Opposite above and below: The Bailey brothers, owners of just one of the many local iron foundries, had a thriving business in Nantyglo, but as they were keen to expand, they blasted a way through the Clydach Gorge in 1822, opening up the Clydach Vale to Gilwern and beyond. As a result the market for their iron products was greatly expanded. The Clydach iron industry started in about 1590, much earlier than at Nantyglo. Work in the area brought men and their families, resulting in the growth of villages such as Gilwern. These two photographs show the village of Gilwern's main street in around 1920, after the closure of the iron industries. Despite this, many people remained in the village and the community flourished.

35438 J.V   GILWERN VILLAGE, ABERGAVENNY. (12)

At one time there was a blast furnace for ironmaking close to the village of Gilwern. Dating from 1696, it was still in use as late as 1860. The discovery of minerals in the area brought an influx of families as men came seeking employment. Here is Gilwern on a Bank Holiday in August 1932, with the main road from Abergavenny to Brynmawr as it passes through the village. The Congregational and Baptist chapels can be seen, as can Gilwern School. Major development of the village had not yet taken place.

With places such as Brynmawr, Beaufort and Nantyglo also growing in population, there quickly sprang up a variety of chapels and mission churches. As the community faced the hardships of everyday life the solace and peace offered by religious worship was beneficial to all. The vision and pioneering spirit of the ironmasters soon made this area a veritable hive of activity. This photograph shows a view of Gilwern and the Sugarloaf and was taken from near the railway line on Gilwern Mountain.

Above and below: The main street, Gilwern, around 1910. With the furnaces glowing white with the immense heat, the empires of great ironmasters such as the Crawshays and the Hanbury brothers brought monetary rewards both for the community as a whole and for the owners of the iron foundries. A number of large houses, which are still in existence today, soon began to appear and the history of these houses strongly suggests the power and control that a few industrialists wielded in the locality. Much of the land was owned by the Beaufort estate. The famous Clydach House is but one of many, and has a coat of arms dated 1693. Workers' cottages began to spring up everywhere and Ynys-y-Garth contains fine examples of such dwellings, as do Castle Row and Forge Row.

This 1965 shot of the main road in Gilwern was taken from just above the Navigation Inn which can be seen on the right. On the left-hand side of the road is the Roadhouse Café. Further on are Mr Don Powell's hardware shop and the Congregational Chapel. There was a lay-by opposite the chapel which remains in use today. This wonderful photograph also includes the Bridgend public house and a number of cars from that period. Five public houses were located within a short distance of the main road.

Pentwyn Farm around 1920, before work began on the Heads of the Valleys Road, when the farm was demolished in the name of progress.

Gilwern's main street during the 1950s. There is a bus stop for Brynmawr on the left-hand side of the photograph and during the 1960s the street boasted a hairdresser and Mrs Price's shop. The registration number of the Morris van is GUY 263. Outside the shop of Mr Ron James (on the right) a delivery bicycle can be seen. The bus stop for Crickhowell was behind the Beaufort Arms in front of the public convenience. During the 1960s the Crickhowell bus came from Brynmawr and was a single-decker; it would turn for Crickhowell around the toilets and stop outside the rear entrance to the Beaufort Arms. Cars and lorries coming into Gilwern from the direction of Abergavenny would at one time turn right opposite the Dell shop to go to Crickhowell, rather than pass the Beaufort Arms before turning right. This practice was discontinued during the 1960s as a result of many minor accidents.

The main street further on as it leaves the shopping area behind. Both photographs capture a wonderful bygone age when road traffic was minimal.

Moving away from Gilwern's main street we see Factory Bridge, which at one time carried the old road to Crickhowell. To avoid this detour, in 1938 a new bridge across the gorge was built some 300 yards away. The waterfall on the left was used to drive a water turbine, which replaced an earlier waterwheel.

A view from the new bridge in the general direction of the old bridge, showing how the gardens slope down towards the River Clydach.

This photograph, sadly of very poor quality, was taken near the Corn Exchange in Gilwern, possibly around 1910. Cheese making was a very profitable industry, so many local women would practise this art to supplement their household income. The trips to the markets at Brynmawr, Abergavenny and Crickhowell by pony and trap and on foot were a great highlight – vendors and purchasers could hone their bartering skills and a good day could be had by all.

A family outside their cottage at Forge Row between Gilwern and Clydach. Notice the family's pig outside the house. The cottages always had a pig in the sty which eventually would become the family dinner. Some of the men made 'yokes' mainly to enable the women to carry goods on their delivery rounds. Sheep shearing involved yet another gathering of the clan, where men did the shearing and the women were responsible for the huge task of feeding the hired gangs.

Gilwern in winter, around 1920. The canal often froze, and ice, snow and freezing conditions made the area hazardous. The village of Gilwern is surrounded by four waterways. From the town of Brynmawr comes the River Clydach, which translated means 'rocky stream'. As the river runs down the Clydach gorge, it gathers momentum and often in times of heavy rainfall can become a raging torrent. The River Baiden flows from Gilwern Hill. As it passes through the farmland on its downward journey it refreshes the fields. After passing under the Heads of the Valleys Road at Aberbaiden roundabout, it flows into the River Usk.

Three miles away from Gilwern is the small market town of Crickhowell, which stands on the east bank of the River Usk. The town has a Norman castle, which was one of thirteen built in the county of Breconshire. Although only a small proportion of the site now remains, both the castle and the town are popular with tourists. The river bridge across the Usk, together with part of the town, is seen in this photograph taken around 1920. The river often bursts its banks and this area has flooded on many occasions. Anglers enjoy trout and salmon fishing here.

Right: A well-known figure in the village for many years was Wesley Paske, who is seen in the uniform of the Royal Army Medical Corps around 1943. He served with distinction during the Italian campaign. Mr Paske gained a Mention in Despatches for distinguished service, which was published in the *London Gazette* on 19 July 1945. After marrying Vera Walters he moved to Gilwern where he took the position as manager of the Co-operative store. Until his death in 1983 he was an active member of the Congregational Church, where he often played the organ.

Below: The wedding of Vera Walters, from Clydach, to Mr Wesley Paske in 1948. Left to right, standing: Christine Davies, Stan Williams, Mabel Williams, Wesley Paske, Vera Walters, Richard Davies, Mabel Lloyd, Jack Walters, Jean Thomas. Seated: Kathleen McIntosh, Keith Williams, Sheila Williams.

Left: Mr and Mrs Paske on holiday around 1962. The couple enjoyed a number of holidays in the British Isles, although neither of them learnt to drive and they always relied on public transport. Mr Paske also served on the Parish Council and would always stand up for what he believed was right. The couple were deeply religious and often campaigned for activities within the community.

Below: Mr Wesley Paske with his staff, pictured in the Co-operative store, Gilwern during the early 1960s. Early closing days for the store were Monday and Thursday. The shop also closed for lunch between 1 and 2 p.m. and close of business for the day was 5.30 p.m.

Above: After Mr Paske's retirement from the Co-operative store, he and his wife were required to move out of their home, Wilma, in Gilwern's main street as the house belonged to the company. Mr Paske is standing outside the property the couple subsequently purchased; the two photographs were taken in 1971.

Below: Part of Mr and Mrs Paske's house prior to the substantial alterations that were made. The house next door belonged to Mr and Mrs Charlie Jones, whilst glimpsed to the right is the well known Guest House which Mrs Mary James ran for thirty-eight years. The house and front garden of Mr and Mrs Ted Sharman can be seen in the foreground.

Another well-known grocer of Gilwern, Mr Ron James, who ran the Mace store. Mr James was born in 1919 and came from Tredegar. Conscripted into the army at the outbreak of the Second World War, he served with the Royal Engineers. One of the many evacuated from Dunkirk, he later returned to the war and was captured at Tobruk. He then spent a number of years in various prisoner of war camps before returning to Britain in 1945. After marrying a local girl, Mary Moss, the couple purchased the store and ran it until his retirement at sixty-five. Mr James passed away in 2001. Mrs James served for a time on the Community Council and at one time, before her marriage, lived with her parents at Station Terrace, Gilwern.

Opposite above: The finished house of Mr and Mrs Paske in 1973. After Mr Paske's death his wife Vera remained in the property until she died in 1993.

Opposite below: Mrs Paske was an active member of the Women's Guild for many years. The Guild's 50th anniversary tea, left to right: Mrs M. Jones, Mrs S. Powell (President), Mrs V. Paske (Treasurer), Reverend E. Powell, Mrs A. Jones (Secretary).

Above: As early as the 1930s a plan for a new road, to be called the Heads of the Valleys Road, was proposed to help ease the heavy congestion on the Black Rock Pitch. The road, which was 24 miles long, was finally completed in 1962 after the closure of the Abergavenny to Merthyr railway and now covers part of the old railway line. At the time of its opening it was considered to be a remarkable feat of road engineering. The building of the Heads of the Valleys Road involved the demolition not only of a number of cottages but also of a farmhouse dating back to the sixteenth century and a mission church between Gilwern and the sale yard. As the work progressed the construction of a number of retaining walls, underpasses and bridges was required. The building of the new road is underway while the demolition of the farmhouse begins.

Opposite above: Mrs Sally Powell, the Guide leader who founded the 1st Gilwern Girl Guides, pictured with her assistants.

Opposite below: On the occasion of Mrs Powell's retirement after thirty-five years' service, left to right: Mrs Tinsley (the new leader), Mrs Powell, Mrs N. Stockham, Miss L. Evans.

In 1982 a large fall of snow covered the area. The top photograph shows the canal in the village at the time of the snowfall, and below is the same area later in the year.

Above and below: More images of the snow in 1982, this time the main street of Gilwern. Up until the early 1990s large snowfalls were commonplace but people were still able to get about.

Above and below: The village in 1982. Looking towards Abergavenny and the Corn Exchange public house.

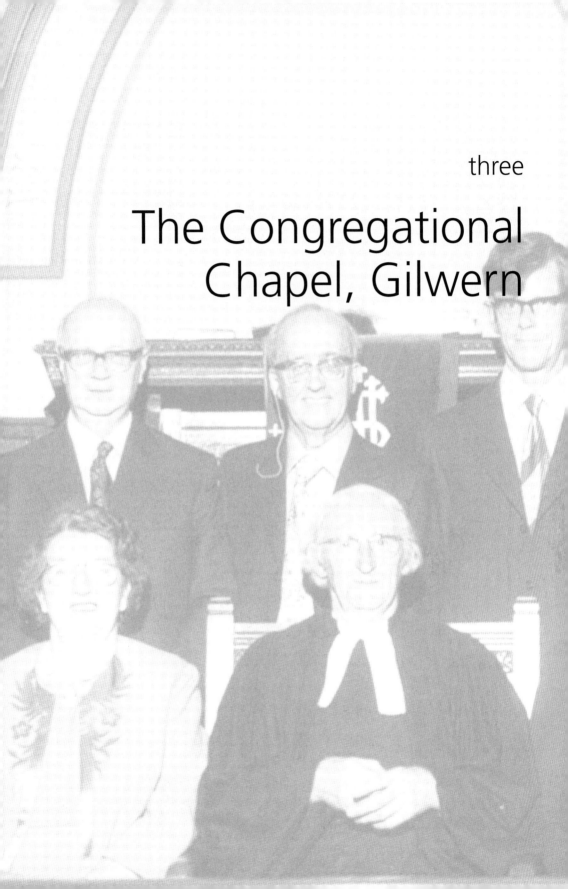

three

The Congregational Chapel, Gilwern

Above: The small communities of the village and the surrounding area had their 'fun and games' long before industrialization came to the valley. This centred very much around the large-family way of life where everyone learnt useful skills and crafts. From the close harmony singing of the choirs to the brewing of beer, each event would have a place in the community. Prior to the days of rugby and football, the populace would enjoy spectating at organised bouts of 'bare fist' fighting. Bread making was a special craft and necessary to the family diet whilst sheep milk was a lifesaver to the weak child. As a result of the efforts of only thirty-four members of the congregation the task of building the Congregational Chapel in Gilwern's main street began in 1880. The foundation stone was laid by Mrs Thomas of Balmoral House, Newport in May 1886, the builder being recorded as Meadow of Abergavenny. The completed chapel was opened for worship in December 1886.

Opposite: The first full time minister was the Reverend J.M. Jones who retired in early 1896, being replaced by Mr Owen Griffiths. January 1903 saw the induction of Reverend Josiah Davies who continued the good work until his sudden death in January 1912. Ordained in November 1912 and photographed on 12 April 1915 was Mr Thomas Jeremy of Carmathen College.

The Reverend Lewis H. Davies was inducted as Minister in January 1924. As a result of the First World War, finances were under great strain and like many others at this time, the chapel struggled to survive. From July 1932 to the end of 1940 Mr Lewis H. Howells was the Minister. During the war the chapel carried on despite the difficulties and as the end of hostilities approached Mr Edgar C. Powell of Memorial College Brecon was ordained Minister in July 1945.

A fine harvest festival display in the chapel in around 1920. These events were well attended with local children enjoying the afternoon harvest festival service and the pleasure of donating the gifts.

Right and opposite: Under the guidance of the Minister and elders of the Congregational Chapel in Gilwern, a Manse Fund was started in August 1943. In order to raise the funds required many members loaned sums of money interest free. Mrs M.E. Powell of Clydach Farm, together with her family, gave the site for the Manse in Station Road in memory of the late Alderman Wilfred Powell, a great and loyal officer over many years. The architects were Messrs J. Merton Jones and Sons, and the builder Mr Llewellyn Pickering. In April 1949 Professor John Evans of Brecon opened the Manse. By 1952, the Manse debt had been erased thanks to the generosity of members and friends under the leadership of the treasurer Mr Thomas Hadley and the secretary Mr Bert Jones. These photographs show the opening of the Manse, Mr and Mrs Powell's home. The Manse is still in use today as the minister's home.

Reverend Edgar Powell with his wife Sally shortly after they arrived in Gilwern in 1945. They are with the deacons of the chapel at that time. From left to right, back row: W. Powell, T. Hadley (Treasurer), G.Thomas, J. Williams, A. Jones (Secretary), E. Hammond. Front row: B. Jonathan, M.S. Powell, S.Powell, Reverend E.C. Powell, R. Parry, L. Powell, S. Jones.

The Elders of the chapel, probably during the late 1950s. From left to right, back row: C. Jones, R. Williams, R. Jones, W. Paske, H. Howells, R.J. Hadley, B. Jones. Front row: M.E. Powell, L. Powell, Reverend E.C. Powell, S. Powell, E. Hammond.

The souvenir programme of a harvest thanksgiving service broadcast on the Welsh Home Service from the Congregational Chapel, Gilwern, on 5 October 1952.

Congregational Church, Gilwern.

Broadcast Service

of

Harvest Thanksgiving

Conducted by

The Rev. Edgar C. Powell

Minister of the Church.

SUNDAY, 5th, OCTOBER 1952.

7.45 — 8.25 p.m.

Welsh Home Service.

———

Organist ...... Miss Frances Jones

Conductor ...... Mr. Wesley Paske

Please take this leaflet home with you.

A. A. Harding, Printer, Tredegar.

The souvenir programme to celebrate Reverend Edgar Powell's twenty-one years as minister. This event took place on 26 May 1966 in Gilwern's village hall.

CONGREGATIONAL CHURCH

GILWERN

Souvenir Programme

To celebrate 21 years service

to the Church and Community by

Rev. and Mrs. E. C. Powell

1945 - 1966

Village Hall,

26th May, 1966,

7.0 p.m.

G I L W E R N   C H U R C H   N E W S

DECEMBER, 1964.

-o-o-o-o-o-o-o-o-o-o-o-o-o-o-o-o-o-o-o-o-o-o-o-o-o-o-o-o-o-o-o-o-o-o-o-

CHRISTMAS MEETING: The expression "out of sight out of mind" is rather one of doubt - or of fear - than of a belief or conviction. The soul surely has eyes that can see the object it loves, through all the intervening darkness of winter - of sorrow - of parting. The first Christmas was delayed - or rather deferred for a time - and when it came how many "wise" knew about the event? How many folk of this age are aware of such a meeting - the meeting of God and man? Only Christians know of the real joy of this meeting, because they reap from this union of hearts both a way and a worship which brings a happy communion with God Himself. The middle wall of partition dividing the Christian family was - so we are told - broken down - but has it gone for ever? Church people may not be united - but Christians are - the people of God are one - because of a meeting - because of the Christmas meeting.

FLOWERS:

Dec. 13th	Mrs. P. Wiggett.	Jan. 17th	In memory-Mr. & Mrs.
20th	Mrs. E. Walters.		Powell, Miss G. Powell
25th	The Sunday School.		& Miss Bevan.
27th	The Sunday School.	24th	Mrs. K. Allen.
Jan. 3rd	In memory-Mr. Rhys Jones.	31st	Margaret's Birthday.
10th	Mrs. S. Withers.	Feb. 7th	Mrs. M. Ambler.
		14th	Mrs. L. Coles.

BIRTHDAYS: JANUARY: 3rd Carl Gunning, Grayson Jones; 4th Karl Watkins; 6th Ann Sharman; Helen Sophia Williams; 8th Ruth Elizabeth Edmunds; 9th Gareth Hodges; 11th Raymond Jones; 12th Clive Thomas and Phillipa Jones; 13th Stephen Charles Llewellyn; 19th Neil Evans.   Many Happy Returns of the Day.

COMMUNION PREPARATION:

December:	Mrs. W. H. Paske.
January:	Mrs. Edith Edwards.
February:	Mrs. Marion McKelvie.

THANKS: For the flowers given to the church during November by - Mrs. P. M. Thomas, by the family of late Mrs. J. Hammonds, Mrs. E. Thomas, Mrs. K. Thomas, and Mrs. Williams, The Firs. All were given to hospitals or sick friends.

An extract from the church news magazine for December 1964 makes interesting reading.

Above: Andrew and Christopher Moss outside their home in Station Road, Gilwern, on their way to present a 30lb pumpkin to the minister. Mr Don Powell, who ran the local hardware store in the village, made the cart they are using.

Right: The December 1964 issue of *Congregational Monthly*, featuring Christopher and Andrew Moss in the porch of the Congregational Chapel as they present the pumpkin to the Reverend Edgar Powell. The church also ran a very successful Sunday School and children very often attended the Sunday morning worship during the 1960s and '70s. Before the sermon they would leave the main service and congregate in the vestry where a short lesson would take place. Mr Maynard Ambler of Birch Bank Cottage, Gilwern, would often conduct this and his three children Ruth, Simon and Stephen were regular visitors to the church at this time. Mr Ambler passed away in 1977.

Above: Mr and Mrs Powell in the vestry of the Congregational Chapel, Gilwern, attending a surprise event in their honour.

Left: In 1979 the Reverend E. Powell was featured in a local newspaper. This was the cartoon drawing of the minister which was used to illustrate the article.

Above and below: The wedding anniversary of local lay preacher Alan Jordan and his wife. The celebration took place in the vestry of the Congregational Chapel, Gilwern, and was attended by many well-known locals. Mr Jordan worked at ROF Glascoed for many years.

The elders of the Chapel in 1970. From left to right, back row: C.H. Combes, G. Judd, D. Hawkins, M. Ambler, J. Jones, W.H. Paske. Front row: R.J. Hadley, V. Paske, E. Powell, S. Powell, M. McKelvie.

The 1975 Girl Guides' nativity play in the Congregational Chapel, Gilwern, which by that time had become known as the United Reformed Church.

four

Clydach

This large pillar of rock on the skyline above Gilwern is known in Welsh as Carreg Fawr or Carreg Bica, but in English as The Peaky Stone or The Lonely Shepherd. Local folklore tells how the tenant at nearby Ty Isaf Farm was so cruel to his wife that she threw herself into the Usk and drowned. For his sin, the man was turned into a pillar of stone, but every year on Midsummer's Eve he goes down to the banks of the Usk to search for his wife, plaintively calling her name in vain. By dawn he has always returned to his lonely vigil. It used to be the custom to whitewash the stone so that it could easily be seen when it walked on Midsummer's Eve. The photograph shows the wonderful view across the Usk Valley towards Crickhowell and Abergavenny, which can be seen on a clear day from The Lonely Shepherd.

Opposite above: The small hamlet of Black Rock, prior to the construction of the Heads of the Valleys Road. From Brynmawr towards Gilwern, the magnificent spectacle of the Clydach Gorge stretches past Black Rock hamlet and on through the village of Clydach. At less than half a mile wide and under four miles long, the gorge cuts downwards from 1,100ft above sea level to 400ft at Gilwern. Here the valley opens out and the River Clydach reaches the River Usk a mile below, at Glangrwyney. The valley possessed natural assets which invited early industrial exploitation, which included iron ore and woodland to provide timber for the charcoal furnaces. There was also the advantage of fast streams to supply power for waterwheels.

CLYDACH

A view of Clydach and the school from the south side of the village. This photograph dates from around 1920 and whilst the village spanned two hillsides, the Heads of the Valleys Road had not yet arrived to divide the village in two.

As iron-making in the Clydach Gorge expanded, and with the increased exploitation of coke as a fuel, the need for rapid development of houses and other buildings in the village of Clydach quickly followed. This 1920s view shows some of the homes built as a result of this expansion. History books indicate that charcoal continued in use at one forge for many years and the village of Clydach was able to withstand, for a short period of time at least, the competition from other more established iron-making centres in the main coalfields of South Wales. Although all the required raw materials and sources of energy for iron-making were to be found within the valley, they still had to be brought together for processing.

As it grew, the community attracted people with many interests to the area, choirs and bands being amongst the main interests at this time. The men of the Clydach Band famously won the Eisteddfod at Abergavenny in 1913. This was no mean feat for a small village at this or any other time.

Above and below: Manpower was urgently required for all types of work, including the provision of well-graded routes for the transport of materials along the steep, gullied sides of the Clydach Valley. The industrial potential of the area was vast and it was soon realized that good systems of transport would be needed to take the products further afield. In time, this included the Clydach Railroad, built in 1794, followed by the canal and by 1860, the railway. With the expansion of the village, schools and chapels for the inhabitants of the area were required. Above is Clydach School and below are pupils and members of staff in around 1900.

This view of Clydach South, taken around 1930, shows the steepness of the hillside on which the village was built. The road, which can be seen clearly in the picture, descends from Clydach station towards the road from Brynmawr located on Clydach North side which met at the pipes. On the way the road passed by the Cambrian public house, Bath Row and the Welfare Ground. We can clearly see that prior to the opening of the Heads of the Valleys Road, Station Road as it was known had at one time veered in a U-shape towards the old ironworks.

The Old Forge, Gilwern. 1611.

The ruins of the old forge, Gilwern. This points to a time in the history of Clydach when this pretty valley flashed with the glow of furnaces and resounded to the noise of wheels and machinery. Now all is silent, much of the site of the Clydach Ironworks, including the offices, having been dismantled around 1960. The ironworks were built in around 1790 by John Hanbury, who was a son of Capel Hanbury of Pontypool but records indicate that by 1830 they were owned by Messrs Frere & Co. In 1841 there were reported to be over 1,300 people employed at the works; these included 133 children under the age of thirteen. The date of the photograph is around 1920 and many changes to the area have occurred since.

Clydach Valley.

With the ironworks in full production and the Clydach Gorge echoing to the noise of the iron forges, many men were required to work on the sites. This not only included the men of Clydach and Gilwern but also men from Brynmawr. Here we see a view of the Clydach Valley from Clydach South side.

GLYDACH

There was an urgent need for clothing for all in the community. Here is a view of the old factory which at one time made Welsh flannel blankets and shirts. The factory site was taken over by Alf Chivers, who was the first man to own a lorry in the village of Clydach, and the yard where he set up his business can be seen. It is just possible to see a lorry and a bus belonging to the rapidly expanding Chivers Transport company in the yard in the lower centre of the picture.

The route of the Abergavenny to Merthyr railway line as it climbs up the gorge can be seen here. Also visible is the lime works, built after 1821, which produced vast quantities of lime for the ironworks and the quarry, where around thirty men were employed in 1896. Nowadays it is perhaps hard to believe that there was a time when there were three blast furnaces in the area for smelting the ore. Two forges were used to convert the pig iron into bars, processing approximately 100 tons per week, using around 300 tons of coal.

This photograph, taken from below the site of Clydach football field, shows Blantyre, the home of Harry McIntosh, on the left and the home of the Thomas family next door. The date is not known but in all probability is around 1920 and was prior to the building of the football field and children's play area.

The Welfare Hall in Clydach, which was built in 1933, served the community for many years.

Here we see a fine picture of the official opening of the hall in 1933. A number of local dignitaries were present, including J. Williams, H. Havard, W. Powell, W. Llewellyn, Mr Daniels, H. McIntosh, W. Pritchard and A. Hughes. The young girl to the left of the picture is I. Allen.

Above and below: Two photographs of Clydach football team during the 1950s. The top one shows Clydach AFC in 1950/51. At that time the team were Abergavenny League and District Cup winners. The lower photograph shows the team during the 1954/55 season. The captain in both these photographs was Harold Price, a well-known and much respected person in the area. Harold gave valiant service to the community in many ways and was also known for his singing ability. A number of men from the village of Clydach can be seen, including George Norman, Eddie Williams, Lance House, George House, Jack Evans, Billy Hartson, Ron and George Brace, Sid and Charlie Parry, Elwyn Morris, John George, Ken Price and George Smith.

Clydach AFC later disbanded, but was re-formed in 1977 under the managership of Alan Dance. Members of the squad at that time included M. Brown, L. Brown, W. Brown, C, Cox, C. Dobbs, B, Norman, B. Lewis, D. Edge, J. Price, B. Fury, P. Smith, B. Nuth, P. Pritchard, N. Falkner, P. Thomas, R. Emery and M. Walsh.

Here we see an undated view of Clydach North which includes the Wesleyan Methodist chapel. The first couple to be married at this chapel were Olive Mabel McIntosh and Jack Walters on New Year's Day 1902. Although the chapel was built a number of years previously it had not been granted a licence to solemnize marriages until this date.

Elaine Evans and John Williams standing behind the counter of the General Stores, Clydach, on 30 April 1962, when Mr Williams took over the shop. The customer facing them is Anne Eynon. Mr Williams was born in September 1898 and continued working until the age of eighty-two. His working life included a number of years' service on the railway, together with time spent in the local coal mines. He passed away in 1988 aged nearly ninety. The shop finally closed in December 1982.

The Rock and Fountain public house, seen on the left, was built around 1873 and still stands today. Dances were frequently held here and it was always a popular local pub. Rock House can be seen in the middle of the photograph. Built in 1873, this was the home of the author between 1973 and 1982. The course of the Clydach Railroad can be seen on the right.

The old lime kilns of Black Rock Limeworks. Next to the kilns is an incline which works its way up the mountainside towards Daren Ddu. This view also includes part of the Black Rock Pitch, the notorious road between Brynmawr and Gilwern. Built as a turnpike road under an Act of Parliament during 1812/13, it was paid for by subscription and tolls. The date of this photograph is not known but it appeared in a book on Breconshire published in 1911. This suggests the date as being around 1910.

Lovis Evans with her daughter Sandra, standing on the old Clydach Railroad, above Clydach School, in 1957. Sandra's father was Jack Evans, who was born in Clydach in April 1913. Mrs Evans (whose maiden name was House) was also born in Clydach. The couple lived all their lives in the village. The marriage produced two daughters, of whom Sandra was the younger; her older sister June was born in 1950. The family lived at Brookwood near to the Wesleyan Chapel.

Here we see, from left to right, Annie Evans, Sandra Evans, June Evans and Lovis Evans. Mr Jack Evans, who was the postmaster in Brynmawr between 1946 and 1961, took the photograph at Porthcawl in 1960. Called to serve his country during the Second World War, Mr Evans served with RAF Coastal Command and later 56 Group Fighter Command. He later worked for the Unemployment Benefit Service until his retirement in 1973. Mrs Annie Evans (grandmother of June and Sandra) was the postmistress in Clydach between 1919 and 1935, receiving a long service certificate for thirty-six years' service. The registration of the 600cc BSA motorcycle combination is JAV 163.

Above: Mr and Mrs Jack Walters, the parents of Mrs Vera Paske, at their daughter's home in Gilwern during the early 1960s. The couple spent most of their lives in Clydach but when they were older they moved to their daughter's home. Jack was born in 1879 and worked at the various pits and quarries in the area. He had a number of interests, including music and was also a member of Clydach St John Ambulance team. The couple lived to celebrate their diamond wedding anniversary. Jack passed away in 1963 and his wife in 1965. They were buried at Abergavenny cemetery.

Left: Here the couple are pictured with Mrs Walters' sisters at the home of Mrs Paske in around 1962. Mrs Evelyn Thomas, on the left, was born in 1892. Her husband Fred was also born in Clydach and both lived to a ripe old age. The youngest sister, Mrs May Davies, passed away in December 1999 aged over 100. Her husband Richard worked for the London & North Western Railway, rising to the position of stationmaster.

Ivor Stanley Williams was born in the village of Brithdir in 1903 but came to live in Clydach at an early age. His parents were publicans and lived in the Station Hotel, Clydach, and later the Rock and Fountain Inn. In 1917, after returning to the village of Brithdir, he started work at Elliott's Colliery, New Tredegar. He retired in 1968 after fifty-one years' dedicated service to the mining industry. By the time of his retirement he had risen to the post of Mines Safety Inspector for Glamorgan and Monmouthshire, working on behalf of the men as a representative of the National Union of Mineworkers South Wales Branch. In his later years Stan, as he was always known, had a great interest in cine photography. He made many films, which he showed to various societies.

This photograph shows Stan giving a film show in 1967 to the Women's Guild at the Congregational Chapel, Gilwern.

The wedding of Ivor Stanley Williams to Olive Mabel Walters in 1927. Left to right: Lilly West, Frank West, Stan Williams, David Morgan, Mabel Walters, and Jack Walters. Seated: Edina Mutlow and Vera Walters.

Stanley Williams with his wife Olive Mabel Walters a few days after their wedding in 1927. Mabel, as she was known, was born in Clydach on St George's Day 1903. The eldest daughter of Mr and Mrs Jack Walters, she and Stan were childhood sweethearts. In April 2003 Mabel celebrated her 100th birthday but sadly passed away in June of that year. After the wedding Mabel moved with her husband to live in the Rhymney Valley, moving to George Street in the village of Brithdir in 1930, where they remained until 1972. Both Mabel and her sister regularly worshipped at the Wesleyan Chapel, Clydach, until their marriages. Both had a musical talent and enjoyed the singing and fellowship of the village.

Harry's second eldest son Alan with his wife Iris and daughter Lorna on a visit to Barry Island. Alan, a well known milkman in the area, who at one time lived at the Sale yard, started the first paper round in Clydach.

A group of regulars from the Rock and Fountain public house during the early 1980s on a visit to the Bierkeller in Bristol. The photograph includes Colin Walbank, Linda Thomas, Stephen Mogford, Richard Thomas, John Price and Gareth Jones.

Opposite above: Harry McIntosh lived in Clydach all his life. Born in 1888, he started work in 1900 in one of the local pits. When the death of Queen Victoria was announced in 1901 the news was conveyed around the country by telegraph, often to the local railway stations. Harry was one of the first to hear the news in Clydach, and passed the news on to many in the village. He married Rebecca Mary Hook, who came from Cardiff, in 1912. The marriage produced five children. Rebecca passed away in 1968. This photograph shows Harry McIntosh with his wife Rebecca, daughter Kath and son-in-law Jim Parker whilst on a holiday in Ireland during the 1950s. A well-respected and popular figure in Clydach and the surrounding area, Harry was offered a place at John Ruskin College, Oxford, but declined. One of seven children, he raised a family whilst studying to improve his position, and became a district councillor after his sixtieth birthday, a position he held for around twenty years. Like many of his contemporaries, he once studied shorthand with the vicar of Govilon Church. The Bible was used in these endeavours as this was the book which most families were likely to possess.

Above: Clydach Quarry in the late 1930s. At this time the quarry was taking on extra labour in anticipation of the forthcoming war. The photograph includes a number of men from Clydach, including the quarry manager Mr D.W. Powell, who ran the quarry between 1926 and 1955, Windsor Weaver, Fred Thomas, Tom Williams, Harry Powell and Harry McIntosh. The previous manager was Mr J.E. Williams (1890-1926). The Clydach and Abergavenny Lime and Stone Co. Ltd worked the quarry. This company had been in business in the Clydach Valley since 1871.

Mr C. Grant, the headmaster of Clydach School, with his teaching staff around 1900. Mr Grant was a well-known and very respected member of the community. In the photograph is Olive Mabel McIntosh, who was born in 1880 in the village of Clydach. As she grew up she studied hard and became a teacher at Clydach School. As was the custom at this time, female members of the teaching staff were required to resign if they married; thus when Olive wished to marry she resigned her position. Her leaving present was a china tea set which she used throughout her married life.

Opposite below: This photograph, again taken in the 1930s, shows a number of local ladies enjoying a picnic while visiting the quarry site. They are Elizabeth Thomas, Vera Walters and Mary McIntosh. Also in the picture is Wesley Thomas who around this time was ordained as a minister. The lorries of the Chivers Transport Company removed a large amount of the stone blasted on the site.

Pupils of Clydach School, around 1916. The First World War was in full swing and the news from the front was often bad. No doubt in order to boost the morale of the children a fun day had been organized by the staff.

Above and opposite below: Two photographs of Clydach School in the 1970s; the one opposite below was taken in 1975. Local members of staff include Mrs Higgs and Mrs Norman. Like many small schools, the help of people from within the local community was appreciated.

Above and below: These photographs show Clydach School celebrating St David's Day (1 March). Born near St Bride's Bay, the son of noble parents around AD 520, Dewi Sant (Saint David) is the patron saint of Wales. After being ordained into the priesthood he undertook missionary journeys, eventually arriving in the Holy Land. Thought to have founded many churches during his lifetime, there is a shrine to him at St David's in Pembrokeshire to which many pilgrimages have been made. St David's Day is traditionally celebrated by schools throughout Wales; the girls enjoy the opportunity to dress in national dress, whilst the boys wear a leek or daffodil. Often the school will have a singsong in the morning and close for the afternoon.

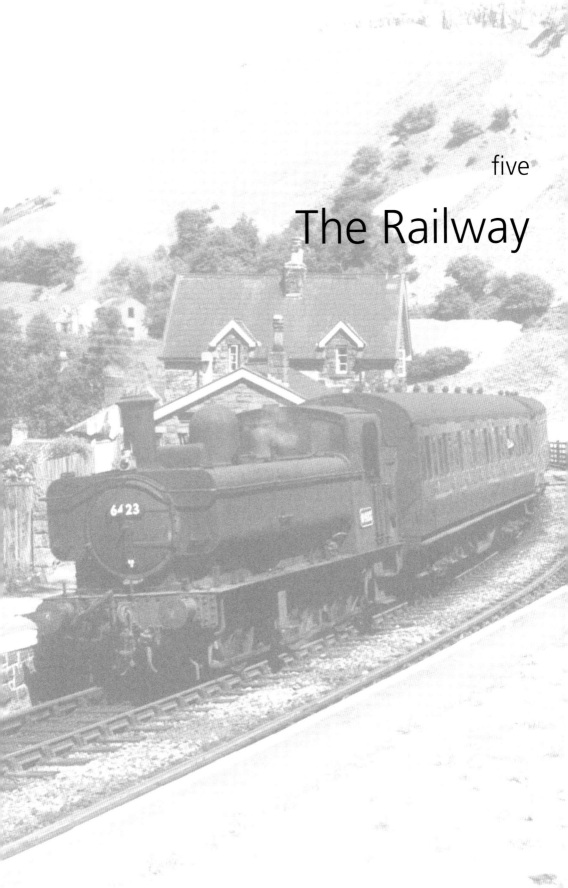

five

The Railway

Gilwern LNWR.

Above: The railway line up the Clydach Gorge rose in an 8-mile ascent to Brynmawr at 1 in 34/37/38, providing breathtaking views for passengers. Here we see a photograph of Gilwern Station, which later became known as Gilwern Halt. Taken around 1910, it shows a train from Brynmawr approaching the station. The route lost its freight trains, both through and local, on 22 November 1954, the traffic being diverted to former Great Western Railway routes. However, contrary to normal practice, passenger services lasted longer, not ceasing until 4 January 1958.

Opposite above and below: The Act for the Merthyr, Tredegar & Abergavenny Railway was passed on 1 August 1859. Within a short period the giant London & North Western Railway, whose directors were keen to gain a foothold in South Wales, had leased the line. The line was opened between Abergavenny and Brynmawr on 29 September 1862. The route was extended from Brynmawr to Nantybwch on 1 March 1864. These two photographs show the last train between Abergavenny and Merthyr on Sunday 5 January 1958 as it approaches Gilwern from Govilon near Ty Gwyn. The train would soon be passing the old Gilwern stone quarry, which closed around 1921, before arriving at the station of Gilwern.

Above: An excellent view of Gilwern Halt building, around 1957. Today, little trace of this forgotten building can be found. Although only about half a mile away from Gilwern village, the climb to the station was steep for passengers.

Opposite above: This picture was taken from one of the carriages of the last passenger train to Merthyr on Sunday 5 January 1958. A number of the local inhabitants of Gilwern turned out to watch the last train pass through. It is very interesting to note that many people from the villages and towns along the route turned out to watch the passing of this train. Perhaps if they had used the service on a regular basis, the trains would have remained for a few years longer.

Opposite below: Pictured here is a pre-1921 westward view of Gilwern Station. As there appears to be a man in military uniform on the up platform it is probable that the picture was taken during the First World War. This excellent picture also clearly shows the curvature of the station and the steps for passengers to use from the road bridge.

Taken in 1993, thirty-five years after closure, mother nature has again got a firm hold and the undergrowth has covered the track bed. During the 1960s the station building on the up platform had been used as a hut for the 1st Gilwern Cubs, but was unfortunately destroyed by a fire in 1969.

The Tunnels—under The Dinas,
Clydach Station. 1602.

Above and below: Clydach Station and the viaduct can be seen in the first of these photographs. The curvature of the viaduct is a fine testament to the Victorian engineers and navvies who built the line. Both photographs show how the line clings to the side of the hill as it twists and turns on the steep climb towards Brynmawr. The final section of the route to Merthyr was opened on 4 June 1879.

An auto train about to depart Clydach Station for Abergavenny in September 1957. This magnificent photograph shows a scene from a bygone age of what was arguably the most scenic railway in Great Britain.

Opposite above: Clydach signal box photographed during the 1950s. Built in 1898, it remained in use until the closure of the line in 1958.

Opposite below: The substantial building on the up line. Once again no passengers can be seen. In reality the stations of both Gilwern and Clydach were a long way from the villages. Change is not always for the best and one can only speculate that if the line had survived another ten years it might have become a tourist attraction.

Opened in September 1933, Gelli Fellen Halt could be found on a tight curve with short staggered platforms. This picture shows the railway line a short distance away from the halt, as the line continues towards Brynmawr. The magnificent view and bleakness of the area is evident and one can only admire the engine men who worked the line during its lifetime.

Opposite above: Once clear of the platform at Clydach Station, trains travelling to Brynmawr entered Clydach tunnels. Emerging once again into the daylight the train would continue on its tortuous route to Brynmawr by running through the Weir Wood, along a ledge overlooking the valley. Here we see the eastern portals of Clydach tunnels, which are two separate small-bore portals. This photograph was taken in January 1958 as the last train approached the tunnel mouths. It is still possible to see the tunnels today.

Opposite below: Here we see Gelli Felen tunnels with a Webb 0-6-2-tank locomotive on a passenger service to Abergavenny around 1930. These gallant locomotives worked on the line for around fifty years.

A rear view of the gorge from a passenger train heading towards Brynmawr in 1951, as it approaches Gelli Felen tunnels. The tight curves of the line as it steadily climbed towards Brynmawr are evident but perhaps not so evident is the fact that the small hamlet of Black Rock lies across the other side of the valley. Below the steep descent of the hillside, the River Clydach can be found and one can only wonder if the passengers who travelled the line prior to its closure gave any thought to the legends of the valley below. It is said that Shakespeare visited the area and wrote *A Midsummer Night's Dream* in a cave below the gorge.

Leaving Gelli Felen tunnels the same train has continued to climb in the darkness and is now approaching Gelli Felen Halt.

Brynmawr Railway Station, which, at 1,200ft above sea level, could arguably be called the coldest station in Great Britain. This photograph, taken in 1938, shows a Webb Coal Tank en route to Abergavenny with a local passenger service. Although a Webb Coal Tank has been preserved, as yet a Super D is not running. The old station site has now been completely redeveloped and no trace of the railway at this location can be found.

This view of Brynmawr Station shows the huge complex of the station site. To the left is the bay platform, which was used until 5 May 1941 for a passenger service to Pontypool. The provision of a covered bridge at this site was much appreciated by passengers.

The last train to Merthyr arrives at Brynmawr. It is clear that many people turned out to see this sad event. The day was very well recorded by photographers and film makers. Both types of locomotive used on the last train were the mainstays of motive power during the time of the line's existence. Although the Webb Coal Tank (the leading locomotive) has been preserved, as yet a Super D (the second locomotive) has not achieved the same standard of preservation.

Buried in Llanfoist cemetery (which the line passed on its way to Brynmawr) is Crawshay Bailey, who was born in Yorkshire. This remarkable man can arguably be considered to be the prime motivator in the building of the Heads of the Valley line. Well known for his knowledge of mining and iron-making, he was also a Member of Parliament representing the Monmouth borough between 1852 and 1868, as a Conservative.

Crawshay Bailey's credits include owner, ironmaster, canal director and first chairman of the Merthyr, Tredegar and Abergavenny Railway Company. He was well known for his promotion of canal and railway development, and his place in Welsh history is assured. Towards the end of his life he lived at Llanfoist House near to the railway line. He died in January 1872 without seeing his vision of the railway to Merthyr completed. Another view of the last train from Abergavenny to Merthyr, pictured at Brynmawr Station on Sunday 5 January 1958.

This view of platform 4 was taken after the closure of the line to Abergavenny. Brynmawr retained a railway passenger service to Newport until 30 April 1962. Platform 4 was a bay platform which until 1958 was used by the Newport trains.

six

Brynmawr
Comprehensive
School

The town of Brynmawr (which means 'big hill' in Welsh) was at one time considered to be the largest town in the county of Breconshire. Around 1910 the population was recorded as being 7,000. Brynmawr stands on the Llangynidr Limestone Mountain, at an elevation of 1,200ft above sea level, and is the highest town in South Wales. The position of the town is bleak and exposed, and this often caused the town to be cut off in periods of heavy snowfall. Until the mass closure of the coal mines in the 1980s, many of the men from the town were employed in the local mining industry. Others found employment with Dunlop Semtex or the Tuff Shoe Factory which made the town a centre of local trade. Prior to the opening of the Heads of the Valleys Road in the early 1960s the main road to Abergavenny was the old Black Rock pitch. This photograph shows the road climbing away from the Bridgend public house, prior to its descent down the Clydach Gorge.

Opposite below: A drawing of Brynmawr County School as it looked in 1898. The school had formally come into being on 20 January 1897, the original school rooms being located in the Methodist Chapel in Orchard Street and the English Wesleyan Chapel in Alma Street, Brynmawr. The number of pupils recorded at this time was forty-one.

Above: A view of the Market Square in Brynmawr in 1953. This would appear to be a very busy day, with local buses very much in evidence. The old name of Brynmawr was Wain Helygen (The Marsh of the Willow), derived from a piece of land known as the Marshes. Many pupils who attended Brynmawr Comprehensive School will agree with that statement, as the land on which the school was built was very boggy.

Brynmawr County Intermediate School.

Mr T.L. Williams was the first headmaster of Brynmawr County School. Born in 1869, he was the son of a minister in the town of Hirwaun. After attending the local school, he attended Pengam Grammar School. This was followed by further education at Llandovery College. He later passed the Oxford Local Examination with the highest honours, and also the London Matriculation examination. After studying at Aberystwyth for three years, he obtained a London BA with honours. After teaching at Rochester and his old school Pengam he became headmaster at Brynmawr in 1897. He was popular with both staff and pupils and gave excellent service to the school, retiring on 31 January 1929.

The new headmaster was Mr T.W. Price who took up the position on 1 February 1929. During his term of office a number of improvements to the school took place. During the year 1929/30 the prefect system was introduced, D.L. Jones being appointed head prefect for the boys and N. Weaver for the girls.

Report books were first used in January 1931 and four more classrooms, a masters' room and two cloakrooms were brought into use while the prefects were given their own rooms. Violin classes were taking place and in 1932 a school orchestra was formed. Further improvements continued with the installation of electric power and light in 1935. Sadly, during 1937 Mr T.L. Williams, the former headmaster, passed away. A memorial was unveiled in the School Hall on 12 September 1938 by Mrs Ethel Williams. During that year Wilfred Neat won the first State Scholarship in the school's history. The provision of mid-day meals began at a cost of 1s 6d per week. Sadly in September 1939 Great Britain entered into another worldwide conflict and again the school saw many former pupils in action, with many paying the ultimate price.

Two pupils gained Welsh Secondary Schools Rugby Union caps. The first was Hector Mckelvie in 1928, followed by Joseph Pritchard in 1938. On 5 April 1939 the school held a concert at the Market Hall, Brynmawr, which included a play. Another pupil, Muriel Gore, won a State Scholarship as the school went from strength to strength.

The school badge for Brynmawr County School is shown. When the school became a comprehensive in 1964 the badge remained almost the same with the word 'County' being replaced with 'Comprehensive'. During the fifty years between 1897 and 1947 the school enrolled approximately 3,000 pupils.

The Great War of 1914/1918 took a severe toll on the young men of the area. Opposite is reproduced the Roll of Honour for those pupils who fought, and on the left is the jubilee magazine cover for Brynmawr County School which celebrated fifty years in 1947. The magazine gives an interesting insight into the school before the First World War and up to 1947.

The Roll Of Honour
Brynmawr Grammar School

First World War, 1914-1918. Roll Of Honour

Members of Staff

Jenkyn Williams	Richard P. Adams

Pupils

Wilfred Calloway	Stephen Colin	Alcwyn Evans
David John Evans	Nicholas Griffiths	Walter Harris
Herbert Howell	William James	Llewelyn Morgan
Morley Neat	William Phillips	Brinley Price
Gordon Rumsey	John Sutherland	Donald Taylor
George Taylor	Idris Thomas	Christopher Weale
Percy Weeks	Morgan Williams	

First World War, 1914-1918. Distinctions Gained:

Tom Trumper – Military Medal	George Dover – Military Medal
Leslie Perrott – Military Medal	Tom Price – Military Cross
Andrew Provan – Commended for Gallant Conduct	

Second World War, 1939-1945. Roll Of Honour

Jack Ballinger	William Booth	Jack Cheese	Arthur Feebury
Joseph Fear	Arthur G. Jones	William Jones	Reginald C. Pritchard
Terence Ransom	Aneurin Roberts	John Rogers	George Rowlands
J.K. Sutherland	Hugh J. Williams	Thomas R. Williams	

Second World War, 1939-1945. Distinctions Gained:

Ralph Brown – DFM	Arthur Downes – DFC, AFC
John Foley – MBE (Mil. Div.)	Thomas L. Jones – DFC
Lyndon Sims – DFC	Mary McDonald Taylor – MBE
Glyn Williams – Mentioned in Despatches	
Rowland D. White – Croix-de-Guerre, Bronze Medal	
Trefor Jones, Brinley Pritchard, Graham P. Rawlings – OBE military division	

Above: Brynmawr Comprehensive School opened in 1964 (the opening ceremony taking place on Wednesday 18 November 1964) when the Grammar School closed. This meant that every child of school age in Brynmawr and the outlying catchment area would now attend one school. The headmaster was Mr T.R. James, the deputy head being Mr S.G. Pearce. The senior mistress was Miss M.D. Jenkins. The school was and still is located on Intemediate Road, Brynmawr, and was considered a very modern and forward-thinking design for that period. At first the headmaster and his staff encountered a number of problems as the school settled down but these were gradually ironed out. Mr James, Mr Pearce and Miss Jenkins are pictured in the middle of this photograph. The school colours were red and green, as the school song has always proudly boasted. The standard dress for the pupils in forms one to three was green. Boys were required to wear green blazers with the school tie and black trousers. The girls wore green pullovers and skirts.

Opposite: This photograph shows some of the pupils attending the school during 1968. Until 1973, when the arrangements were altered, many pupils would have bad memories of school dinners. In those days the prefects were required to serve the younger pupils and on certain tables this often meant going hungry, as the portions were very small. Then, to add insult to injury, you were required to clear the table. Many a young lad quickly learnt to find a table served by the girls. This had two advantages; the girls were pretty, and you got a lot more to eat as the older girls were watching their figures.

In this photograph, taken in taken in 1968, in the second row, seventh from the left, is Welsh rugby international W.H. Raybould, who taught Welsh at the school. Mr Raybould, a former Cambridge blue, was capped ten times for Wales between 1967 and 1970, and toured South Africa with the British Lions in 1968. A popular figure with both staff and pupils alike he also ran the Welsh Society during his time at the school, which was well attended by many pupils.

The boys of Yellow and Blue Houses with some of the teachers of Brynmawr Comprehensive School in 1973. The author can be found in the top photograph, second row, fifth from the left. At this time there were about 700 pupils attending the school. The standard school uniform for the boys at this time included a black blazer and white or grey shirt with the red and green tie. Facilities which could be found at the school at this time included two chemistry laboratories, two physics laboratories and a biology laboratory.

Opposite below: The sports facilities found at the school included two gymnasia, two rugby fields, a hockey pitch and tennis courts. For athletics, there was an excellent cinder running track together with facilities for field events. Prior to the reorganization of the boundaries the school had the honour of holding the County Sports Day in 1972; this normally took place at Brecon. This picture is dated 1968.

More pupils from Yellow and Blue Houses in 1973. The fifth boy from the left in the third row is Neal Matthews from Gilwern who gained a rugby cap for Wales at schoolboy level that year. Neal later played for Ebbw Vale at senior level. The headmaster at the time was Mr Scott Archer, the deputy head Mr Rowley Jones and headmistress Mrs Carol Morgan, and these three can be seen in this photograph. At the time that this was taken Mr Jones was a well known member of the Welsh Rugby Union. Also included is Mr Clive Nock (who at that time was the games master) who grew up in Clydach, Mr Jim Beddow who lived in Gilwern, and Mr John Hopkins who grew up in Gilwern.

Some of the girls and female teachers from Yellow and Blue Houses. The girls in forms 1 to 3 were now required to wear blue skirts and pullovers while older girls often wore black or maroon pullovers and grey skirts.

The top picture shows the remainder of the girls from Yellow and Blue House while the lower picture shows some of the boys from Red and Green Houses. The four houses had first been introduced in 1925 as a result of the reintroduction of school sports, which had been disbanded in 1913. At that time, intensive rivalry between the houses existed and pride in your house was very strong. To win the Eisteddfod on St David's Day or the play competition that was held meant the house was top dog for the year. Even keener rivalry would exist on Sports Day. All new pupils would follow their brother or sister into the same house. As previously mentioned, the sporting achievements from pupils within the school were good during this period. Many of the pupils represented the school in sports events, some also achieving county recognition. A number of the pupils and at least on member of staff represented Gilwern Harriers, who at that time were considered one of the stronger clubs in South Wales at athletics and cross-country running.

Above and below: Here we see more pupils from Red and Green Houses from 1973. Again the headmaster and his deputies can also be seen. The photograph was taken in the playground in front of the school, overlooking the rugby field and running track. Today this area is covered with extra classrooms. The catchment area at the time that the author attended the school was quite specific – pupils would attend Brynmawr Comprehensive from Gilwern, Clydach, Llanelly Hill and the Brynmawr area. Many of the pupils travelled to school by bus and until 1972 the Red and White Bus Company from Brynmawr held the contract to transport pupils. However, at the start of the 1972/73 year R.I. Davies of Tredegar took over. Rees Buses of Llanely Hill transported the pupils from that village. Prior to September 1969 pupils walked up the drive to the school but in that year a turning circle was installed at the top of the drive. Although it must be pointed out that at this time not many sixth form pupils had passed their driving test, no pupil was allowed to park his or her car on school property.

The date was 23 February 1971 and the occasion a great new sporting event – a pancake race. Thirteen pupils dressed up to enter the event and the records indicate that twelve finished. The two winners were Gillian Bush and Brian Williams. The event was apparently declared a great success.

The school hockey team outside the main entrance to the school in 1973. They are, from left to right, back row: Sue Randell, Sian Walbyoff, Jane Gratrix, Sandra Evans, Judith Lambert, Carol Bradfield. Front row: Jane Bradfield, Gwyneth Jones, Catherine Bowkett, Kim Chivers. The games mistress Mrs Morgan coached the team and four of the girls in this picture were selected for the county. They were Carol Bradfield, Catherine Bowkett, Sandra Evans and Gwyneth Jones.

Above: In early 1973 the BBC filmed *The Green Death*, a series of episodes for the *Dr Who* programme. Great excitement revolved around Brynmawr Comprehensive School when the production team arrived to start filming early one Friday morning. As soon as break time arrived, the majority of pupils rushed to the fence overlooking the Control Data factory to watch as the series was made. The author is pictured with Jon Pertwee, sitting in Dr Who's car, WHO 1. Those who were privileged to see the series being made should retain fond memories of a man who went out of his way during a busy filming schedule to pose with many pupils from the school.

Opposite: During the author's time at the school, Brynmawr Comprehensive produced a series of school magazines. This is the cover for the 1971 issue. The magazine cover also gives a clear view of the school as seen from the main rugby field. It was from the rugby field that the famous and often exasperated cry of 'penalty for dull play' could be heard from Mr Nock when taking some of the junior boys for rugby. The magazine proved to be popular with staff, pupils and parents.

BRYNYSGOL '71

Magazine of the
Brynmawr Comprehensive School

Goreu Ymgais Gwybodaeth

BRYNYSGOL

The Magazine of the Brynmawr Comprehensive School 1970 - 71

Staff Representative—Miss J. M. Joshua.

Editor—Raymond Jones.

Advertising Editors—David A. Jones and Adrian Tuck.

Committee—Gail Price, Helen Bush, Alison Cornelius,
Raye Young, Corrin Hartshorn, Janice Dunster, Lynne Roberts,
Robert Chamberlain, Maldwyn Powell, Gareth Owens, Geoffrey Walker.

Editorial

Felicitations fellow philosophers! Once again you see before you in its brand new cover, one of the most sought after (?) publications of our time "BRYNYSGOL", chockful as usual with intellectual journalism (?), useful information, controversial claptrap and JOKES! But enough of this tittle-tattle.

We welcome to the school five new members of staff, Miss Etheridge, Miss Davies, Miss Williams, Mrs. B. Davies, and finally Mr. S. Aylett, a past pupil of the school. We hope Monsieur Marc Ould "ya" oui has enjoyed his stay with us despite the frustrations imposed by "The Times" crossword. (Vous n'etes pas seul!!!)

We should like to thank Mrs. Price, Mrs. Cornwall, Mrs. Tillotson, and Miss Evans, who left us last year, happiness and success in the future. We also wish great success to Mr. T. Craven who left us at Christmas.

Our congratulations to Timothy Lambert on winning an open scholarship to Oxford.

Finally the committee would like to thank the local tradespeople without whose support this "Comprehensive" chronicle could not exist.

So without further hesitation read on!

P.S. From this point onwards any reference to a person or persons alive or "mummified" is purely intentional.

The editorial for the 1971 issue. The staff representative was Miss J.M. Joshua, who was head of the English Department. The editor, advertising staff and committee were all pupils. Mentioned here is the departure of members of staff together with details of new arrivals. Congratulations were in order for Timothy Lambert who gained an open scholarship to Oxford.

School Page

Head Prefects—Timothy Lambert, Susan Kenna.

Senior Prefects—Alwyn Pritchard, Phillip H. Jones, Catherine Teague.

Girls—	Boys—
Lesley Bradfield	Anthony Cole
Gillian Bush	Robert F. Chamberlain
Helen Bush	David Hodgkinson
Alison Cornelius	Stefan James
Marguerite Cottuli de Cothi	David A. Jones
Gail Cowley	Raymond Jones
Lindsay Downey	Nigel Nicholson
Janice Dunster	Paul Noble
Corrin Hartshorn	Gareth Owens
Denise James	Terence Owens
Linda Johnson	Kevin Pick
Anne Jones	Hadyn Sims
Karen Joynson	Ian Thomas
Gail Price	Stephen Wathen
Clare Pritchard	Paul Whitcombe
Lynne Roberts	Thomas Wiggins
Gwyneth Rogers	Michael Williams
Raye Young	Stephen Williams
Pauline Weeks	Maldwyn Powell
Jane Wilce	Adrian Tuck

HOUSE CAPTAINS 1970 - 71

Gwent (Yellow)—
T. Lambert
P. Weeks
Vice-Captain: A. Cole
G. Rogers

Morgannwg (Red)—
R. Jones
J. Dunster
Vice-Captain: S. James
H. Bush

Brycheiniog (Blue)—
N. Nicholson
C. Teague
Vice-Captain: P. Noble, A. Pritchard
R. Young, C. Pritchard

Maesyfed (Green)—
G. Owens
L. Bradfield
Vice-Captain: B. Williams
K. Joynson

A few details from the 1971 edition of the Brynmawr Comprehensive magazine: Anthony Cole and Paul Noble were selected for the Monmouthshire and Mid Wales secondary schools senior XV while prefects for the year 1970/71 as well as house captains were listed. House Assembly took place on a Friday at this time for the pupils in forms 1 to 3. In the case of Yellow House, the meetings were held in the Music Room. Forms 4 to 6 held their House Assembly on a Monday. On Tuesdays, Wednesdays and Thursdays, School Assembly was held in the Dining Hall. At this time Mr Pearce would stand on the stage supervising as the pupils quietly assembled. He would be assisted by members of staff and on no account would talking be permitted. When all were assembled the school would stand and Mr James would walk onto the stage. After a hymn, a short Bible reading would take place, after which any announcements would be made and the assembly ended by 9.15am. The first lesson was of thirty-five minutes' duration whilst all others were forty minutes long.

Brynmawr Comprehensive School

This Book is the Property of the School Governors and must be PAID FOR IF LOST.

No.	Name	Form	Date Issued	Date Returned
	Jane Adams	VI A		
	Phillip H. Jones	6A	27/4/70	
	Christine Jones	VI	10/5/74	

The slip each pupil was required to fill in when taking possession of a textbook. This slip was found on the inside cover of the book.

The author started Brynmawr Comprehensive School in September 1969. He joined many new starters that day in class 1B, the form teacher being Mrs E. Price. Mr S. Aylett became the form teacher for the summer term of 1970. The pupils of 1B were: Clifford Addiss, Nicholas Beynon, Paul Cable, Brian Davies, David Edge, Simon Holder, Neal Matthews, John Meredith, Ian Rodgers, Jonathan Smith, Gary Robinson, Andrew Williams, Elizebeth Aylett, Jane Bradfield, Cheryl Davies, Angela Eckley, Cheryl Gibbs, Karen Hartshorn, Sharon Haynes, Susan Heol, Coleen Kershaw, Susan Kedward, Lynda Paul, Julie Powell, Gaynor Rackham, Mary Roberts, Yvonne Thomas, Sian Turner, Gaynor Walters, Carol Wheeler, Diane Whitney, Lorraine Williams, Lynne Williams.

Mr S.R. Atkins, who was the senior history master at Brynmawr Comprehensive, was dedicated to his job and gave great service to the school through his teaching, running of the library and, on occasions, giving up his spare time to help with cricket practice. His interesting style of teaching was well known by all the pupils he taught. This includes the author, who on a number of occasions was required to remain in detention but this had the required effect and a successful pass in O level history was duly attained. Also seen here is the cover of S.R. Atkins' *From Utrecht to Waterloo*, published in 1965. Many teachers at the school often gave valuable time to run clubs and societies. Whilst all the events were popular with various pupils, arguably the most successful was the Welsh Society. Run by Mr W.H Raybould, the meetings took place on Tuesday evenings at fortnightly intervals and involved the playing of records, dancing and partaking of refreshments. The evening would end around 9.15 p.m. and happy pupils would make their way home. Guest speakers were often invited, as were local groups, one such group being The Reactions.

Above: One of the many churches found around the town of Brynmawr in around 1900. Through music in places of worship and in schools, children were taught to sing from a very early age. This in turn often brought success to the children, school and town. On Saturday 27 March 1971 a party of school children from Brynmawr Comprehensive, supervised by Mrs H. White, set off to the annual Urdd Eisteddfod at Brecon. The outcome of the event was pleasing to all. Jeffrey Thomas and Kevin Wood were placed equal second in the solo for boys under fifteen years; Hilary Davies was placed second in the piano solo under twelve years; Sian Owen was placed second in the Welsh recitation under fifteen; the new Cydadrodd group was placed second in the under fifteen competition; Helen Bush was placed first in the piano solo under nineteen; and Alison Havard was placed second.

This photograph shows the staff of Brynmawr County School in 1960. Many were present at the annual Brynmawr Comprehensive School Christmas Concert on Wednesday 16 December, 1970. The first item was the Junior Choir, conducted by Mrs. O. Griffiths. It featured Jill Davies, who sang an old Welsh carol. Other items included a recorder group, conducted by Mr J.S. Beddow, Mr T.R. James on the piano and Mr E.K. Watkins on the organ, playing a miniature Concerto for Piano. Then came the sixth form choir, with three carols and featuring Anthony Cole and Dawn Plowman singing *Mary's Boy Child*. After the interval came the highlight of the evening, the choir rendering Haydn's *Creation*, conducted by Mr E.K. Watkins, and featuring guest soprano Ruth Coxall. Mr T.R. James was the pianist and Mr D.M. Williams the organist.

Opposite below: A fine panoramic view of Brynmawr, around 1910, when the plan for a comprehensive school was probably not even a dream.

The top end of the Clydach Valley in around 1900. The railway line can be seen on the right. It would be many years before the changes that altered this valley would occur. Brynmawr County School had a school song with words and music written in the 1930s as a result of a competition. The words were by May Taylor, Headmistress of the Brynmawr Church Junior School and the music by Ken Richards, then on the staff of the same school, but later at Rhymney Grammar School. This popular song was sung on many occasions during the school year and is still fondly remembered by former pupils. The words from the chorus perhaps best reflect the song:

School, girls, school! School, boys, school!
Set on a plateau of verdant green,
High on the hills where the air is clean
And the world is spacious, not cramped nor mean,
Up! Up! for the School!

Thanks to the efforts of a number of pupils and many dedicated teachers, the pupils enjoyed many rewarding social activities. Opportunities existed for pupils with interests as diverse as model aeroplanes, debating and photography. While some pupils left Brynmawr Comprehensive breathing a sigh of relief, the vast majority look back on their time at the school with many fond memories. This is particularly true in the case of the author who enjoyed his time at the school immensely. The school has changed considerably since it first opened in 1964, with new buildings added and a number of other improvements. As time goes by it is inevitable the some of the pupils known by the author will have passed away. Whilst it is not possible to mention everyone who is sadly missed from those days long ago, those who were known to the author as friends should be remembered. They are Julie Edwards, Christine Jones, Eryl Morgan, and Keith Mcloy.

seven

Gilwern Cubs

The Cub Scout and Boy Scout movement was founded by Sir Robert Stevenson Smyth Baden-Powell (1857-1941). Born in London and educated at Charterhouse, he joined the 13th Hussars in India in 1876. Promoted to the rank of Major-General in recognition of his defence of Mafeking, he later organized the South African Constabulary. He became a Lieutenant-General in 1908 and was knighted the following year. After founding the Boy Scout movement in 1908, he later helped to set up the Girl Guide movement. Two of the many books he wrote on the Boy Scout movement are *What Scouts Can Do* and *Scouting and Youth Movement*. Today Scouting exists in over 140 countries and the motto 'Be Prepared' serves the organization well. During the 1960s the 1st Gilwern Cub Scouts was run by Mr Ken Thomas of Bryn Glas. For a period of time between 1967 and 1969, Mr Guy Hanney and Mr Keith Bartlett ran the cubs before they were disbanded. Every effort was made to keep the cubs entertained, and one memorable afternoon a visit to the army camp at Cwrt-y-Gollen included a trip over the assault course. This is the author's Wolf Cub enrolment card dated 16 March 1967.

A new 1st Gilwern Cub Pack was formed in October 1970, with Mrs Mavis Herrington of Station Road Gilwern in charge. Her assistant was Mrs Lesley Pugh, together with help from Mrs Margaret Llewellyn, Mrs Iris Bland, Mrs Brenda Watkins and Mrs Jean Green. This photograph, taken on 12 November 1970, shows the Cub Scout Pack as the new era begins.

Above: The Scout Cub Pack pictured in the Village Hall, Gilwern.

Brownies and Cubs plan joint concert for O.A.P.s

THE newly-formed Brownie and Cub packs in Gilwern are to put on an afternoon's entertainment free of charge for the Senior Citizens of Gilwern, on Saturday, December 18, in the Village Hall.

This week the Brownies and Cubs, in pairs, are visiting all the Senior Citizens of Gilwern, inviting them to come along and see the pantomime performed by the Brownies and the Gang Show to be presented by the Cubs. During the next few weeks a lot of hard work is to be put in by the Brownies and Cubs. The pantomime has been specially written for the Brownies by Mr. W. Newrick, of Orchard Close. The Brown Owl, Mrs. Isabel Lloyd, with Mr. and Mrs. Newrick, Mrs. A. Parry and Mrs. B. Sills, are all working very hard to have the pantomime ready in time.

The Cubmistress, Mrs. Mavis Herrington, with her helpers, Mrs. L. Pugh, Mrs. B. Watkins, Mrs. Jean Green, Mrs. Margaret Llewellyn and Mrs. Iris Bland, will have plenty of work to do over the next few weeks planning and rehearsing a show.

It was only decided this week to stage a joint production for the Senior Citizens. The Brownies and Cubs are then holding their Christmas Party, after the pantomime and show. They are to serve light refreshments to their audience, and transport home will be available for those who need it.

At a meeting of the Cubs' fathers in the Corn Exchange, Gilwern, on Thursday evening, there was a very disappointing turn out.

At a meeting of Cubs' fathers, only eight out of a total of 29 were able to attend. However, several of the fathers offered to help in many ways, and some progress was made.

Mrs. Herrington explained that she needed the help of some of the fathers, for some parts of their Arrow badges were too difficult for her and and her helpers to teach the boys. They involved masculine pursuits such as woodwork, science, photography and tying knots to name but a few. There were offers from the fathers present for help in all those stages of the badges. Mrs. Herrington explained that this would not take up too much of their spare time, for she realised that many of them had very little time to spare.

The Rev. E. C. Powell, the County Commissioner for Cubs and Scouts, explained briefly the reasons for forming a parents' committee, and said that it was not intended to form a committee until later next year.

He paid tribute to the hard work put in by Mrs. Herrington and her helpers, and said how grateful he was to them for revitalising the Cub Scouts.

Mrs Lesley Pugh seen with Mrs Mavis Herrington and the Reverend Edgar Powell, Scout Commissioner, receiving her basic Scout Training award in January 1971.

ADULT LEADER

TRAINING AWARD

CERTIFICATE

LESLEY   PUGH.

has satisfactorily attended

BASIC SCOUTER TRAINING

(A) General Information

Date

(B) Practical *Cub Scout*

30/31 Jan/71 Date

Lesley Pugh's certificate.

Opposite below: A newspaper cutting regarding the forthcoming Christmas Concert.

The Cubs pose for a photograph with their leaders in the vestry of the Congregational Chapel, Gilwern, on 12 November 1970. From left to right, back row: R. Withers, J. Evans, I. Reynolds, D. Williams, A. Griffiths, M. Foulkes, R. Lloyd. Middle row: A. Watkins, M. Pugh, G. Morris, M. Hanney, G. Jones, A. Weed, S. Morgan, R. Edwards, -?-. Front row: R. Morrell, M. Herrington, Mrs V. Davies, A.J. Pugh, R. Smith.

Opposite: Gilwern Cubs in around 1971. The re-formed Wolf Cub Pack had started as a result of a local appeal by Mrs Lesley Pugh, who is seen presenting a prize. The total number of Cubs to form the first pack was eighteen.

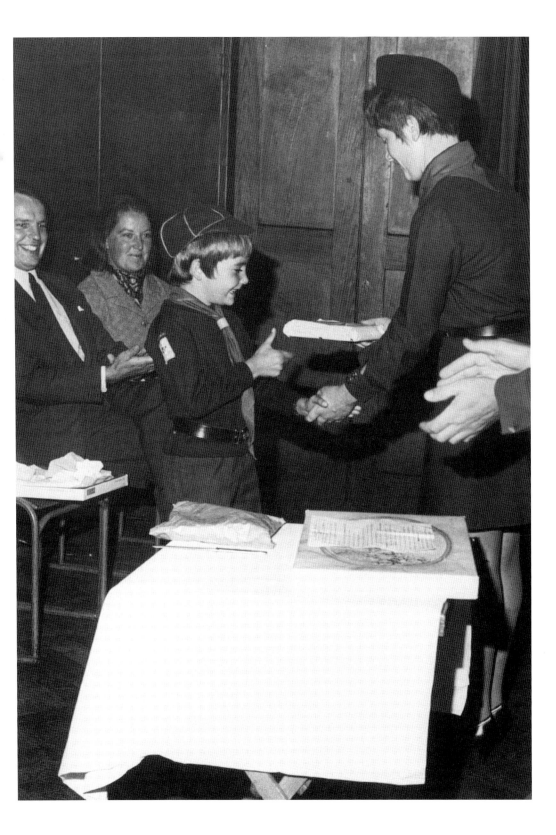

Within a short time the membership grew and lectures were regularly given in the Village Hall. These evenings were well attended and the Cubs were often joined by the Scout troop. This photograph shows some young Cubs as they go about their tasks.

On 6 March 1971 the Gilwern Cubs took part in an eight-mile sponsored walk to Llangattock. The photograph shows the cubs and leaders outside the Congregational Church in Gilwern as they prepare to get under way. Councillor Jack Jones is starting them off. The registration number of the Hillman Hunter at the top left is NAX 935F and Don Powell's shop can also be seen.

A newspaper cutting appeared in the *Abergavenny Gazette* on Friday 12 March 1971, detailing the Cub Pack's achievements. The walk by the Cubs raised over £100. As the Gilwern Wolf Cub Pack grew in strength, many members received awards. During their time in office the leaders of both the Cubs and the Scouts organized various competitions for their members to take part in. This included football with other packs. Although the results did not always go in favour of the Gilwern packs, the days were always memorable. The cubs are on an outing and are standing in front of one of the local coach companies, Rees Coaches of Llanelly Hill.

The Gilwern Cubs in action on the playing fields at Gilwern, taking part in a tug-of-war competition. Local people who can be seen in the picture include John Fletcher from Bryn Glas, who for many years was a football referee, and Mansel Price the assistant Scout Leader. The first Cub on the left is Robert Ackerman from Orchard Close. Robert later played rugby union for Newport and gained the first of his twenty-two Welsh caps on 1 November 1980 against New Zealand at Cardiff Arms Park. He toured with the British Lions to New Zealand in 1983 where he played in the First Test. After gaining his last cap in the 1985/86 season, he spent some time playing Rugby League. Other cubs include David Williams, Nicky Grist (who enjoyed considerable success in the world of motor rallying) and Tim Powell.

The Village Hall, Gilwern, in July 1971: Mavis Herrington with Scout Leader Ken Thomas. The Scouts are left to right: Martin Hanney, Andrew Weed, Rhodri Smith, Stephen Morgan, Gary Jones, and Stephen Hancock. They are taking part in a 'going up' ceremony, having reached the upper age limit for Wolf Cubs. The same night, six new cubs were enrolled. They were Christopher Duncan, Stephen Ambler, Andrew Williams, Ian Wiggett, Stephen Jones and Christopher Jones. During their time in office, Mavis Herrington, Lesley Pugh, Ken Thomas and Mansel Price gave unstinting service to the Cub Scout and Boy Scout movements. Many of those who were members of the organization at that time have fond memories of those days.

Other Welsh titles published by Tempus

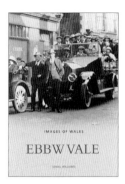

Ebbw Vale
IDWAL WILLIAMS

Ebbw Vale's strong industrial history is well represented in this comprehensive collection of nearly 200 archive images, some of which date from as early as 1900. This book recalls life as it once was before the huge loss of steel industry jobs, and depicts the history of this part of Gwent in terms of its society, its culture and its industry.
0 7524 3209 5

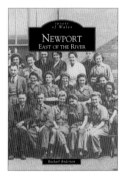

Newport East of the River
RACHAEL ANDERTON

Compiled from the photographic collection held at Newport Museum and Art Gallery, the vibrant history of the town is evocatively captured in over 200 photographs, showing the many changes that have taken place over the last 150 years.
0 7524 2462 9

Merthyr Tydfil The Second Selection
MERTHYR TYDFIL LIBRARIES

Taking the reader on a nostalgic journey into the past this book shows all aspects of life in Merthyr from work and transport to education, worship and recreation. The images in this book will spark many shared memories and show what life was like in a previous age.
0 7524 2684 2

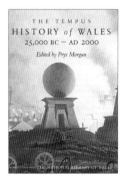

The Tempus History of Wales
PRYS MORGAN

Wales was at the heart of the Industrial Revolution, towns like Merthyr Tydfil driving the engine of the British Empire. The cultural and social divide between modern, industrialized Wales and the traditional agricultural areas is explored within this comprehensive volume.
0 7524 1983 8

If you are interested in purchasing other books published by Tempus, or in case you have difficulty finding any Tempus books in your local bookshop, you can also place orders directly through our website
www.tempus-publishing.com